Gim*p* Crow

Gim*p* Crow

Ken Kowal

TURNSTONE PRESS

Turnstone Press
Artspace Building
206-100 Arthur Street
Winnipeg, MB
R3B 1H3 Canada
www.TurnstonePress.com

Turnstone Press gratefully acknowledges the assistance of the Canada Council for the Arts, the Manitoba Arts Council, the Government of Canada through the Canada Book Fund, and the Province of Manitoba through the Book Publishing Tax Credit and the Book Publisher Marketing Assistance Program.

Cover design: Jamis Paulson
Cover image: *Beaconia by Daylight* (acrylic, mixed media, 2010) by Olya Marko.
Interior design: Sharon Caseburg
Printed and bound in Canada by Friesens for Turnstone Press.

Library and Archives Canada Cataloguing in Publication

Kowal, Ken, 1958–
Gimp Crow / Ken Kowal.

Poems.
ISBN 978-0-88801-375-0

I. Title.

PS8571.O98G56 2010 C811'.54 C2010-904964-0

Mixed Sources
Cert no. SW-COC-001271
© 1996 FSC

this book is for the birds

I went down to St. James Infirmary.
I saw my Sweetheart there.
Lying on a table,
So cold, so white, so fair.
I went up to see the doctor.
"She's very low," he said.
I went back to see my baby
And great God she was lying there dead.

— "St. James Infirmary"

Gim*p* Crow

the crow of my mind

the crow of my mind is
no death row crow
nor some 30s car
toon coon

Gim*p* Cr^o^w's wordy
a bird of ink   who jet
streams nightblack
across my empty
page of mind
smooth as myth

one mask i'm under
wear so i be other
so i can empty
the small
cage of self
        wing
                this body
                 be
                     hind

Gim*p* Cr^o^w introduces himself

Name's Gim*p* Cr^o^w
No Mother Goose
Say all I know
Axe cut lie loose

Love Ol Lady
Best hen there is
Poet make me
Dumb talk like this

Kowal's poetry
Is for the birds
No sense why be
Just us fowled up words

Promise I'll keep
Sweet bye-and-bye
When you fall asleep
Pluck your third eye

letting go

Gim*p*'s a trick i
ease silly fool with my
-self again i gain again

throwing the voice
making air speak

this crow i mind
parrot on shoulder
sees words be
writ then read

O black muse
shell my egg O

prologue

there's this crow i've seen late
-ly scrounging our neighbour-
hood. bad leg. hops a
-cross grass or street, leans
over awkward and sticks
out his bum
                    -leg as if it were
                    a cane.

the grackles give chase
—a flock of Keystone Kops—
the crow knows he's The Tramp,
skidding round sharp corn
-ers, quick blur.

next scene:
                    crow spreads
                                        black wings, opens
his beak scissors-wide. The Director yells:
CAWT   and the crow's jaws snap
shut, clapboard-quick.

then, as the light goes down
The Tramp duds fall
magically, before a black and
white sunset, elm-wind applause.

hiatus

Took big long break.
Where to go? Gim*p* Crow
Don't know what ain't
Still no go

Why limit way?
Four syllables only?
Can hear ya say:
Rhyme's pretty dull

Plenty full doubt
Progress real slow
If written out
It's half-done crow

cock of the walk

Now hirsute Gim*p* Cr^{o}w
Ain't he right handsome?
Sports basic black
Suit'll've to last him

Cakewalks ❍l Lady
Winds up down town
Broad ways elm shady
Squashed squirrels abound

❍l Lady squawks: *Dry*
Guts: stringy. Blood's flat.
Flesh: fresh. No *fly*.
Spect me *eat* that ?

Gim*p*'s leg jerks *CLOUT*
Big toes a twitchin
Done took ya out
Can ya can your bitchin ?

Gim*p* Cr°w's nightmare

oh look now how Gim*p* struggles again
-st his leg to be free   a wh-
ale of a dark beer belly dance
inhaling smells to die for:
apples, oranges, pears,
cherries, a melon

see how Gim*p*'s wings
beat himself silly
wants to leave his bum
-leg be-
hind, empty his shit
-ty cage of bone   sweet
blood flesh traps

and oh
there o
-kay there goes Gim*p*
off again
asleep-flyin
up to no good
night

the itch

When Gim*p* the Crow
Gets a BC cravin
Blows home like snow
Calls Cawsin Raven.

Ol Lady: *Heard*
That bird's oil slick.
Why leave your murder
For a dumb parliament kick?

Gim*p*'s un'stood nuff
Won't hear no more.
Yells: *Go get stuffed.*
I'm off for shore.

Where coast is clear.
Streams: dead salmon,
Fresh killed deer.
Ol Lady: *damn him.*

Caws Rave is, sigh,
Plenty full of tricks:
Fly through a pigsty
No shit would stick.

separation

Girl ya don't:
                    Yin my yang
            Beak my lang
Cool down ang

Girl ya don't:
                    Bucket well
            Clap dumb bell
Heaven hell

Girl ya don't:
                    Quaff down dregs
            Twitch my legs
Clutch close eggs

Girl ya don't:
                    Cure my ache
            Beak toothless snake
Ya pure miss take

Girl ya don't:
                    King my kong
            Sing our song
Or bounce, so: *so long*

daybreaks

Now Gim*p* the Cr^ow
Don't want no trouble
Just his daily dough
Nut dip mournin puddle

Roosts round Robin's
With the gulls and grackles
Squabbles over day-olds
Bin dives beak full

Don't got no job
Ain't exactly lookin
Don't crack open *The Sun*
Might find somethin

Ain't hurtin no one
Wouldn't help a fly
Another night done
Glad he didn't die

the plan

Now Gim*p* Crow
Hates kerfuffle
Lady's tight brow
Feathers a ruffle

Time left sad nest
And hip-hop freight
Full head steam West
Hope bad love ain't

why did the crow cross the continent?

            fed up with snow
driftin   near   white
cold   wind blowin
food frozen hard

all week the weak
    half-died
and the strong
    less sure

all cooped up   bein
slowly driven kin
-da nest-happy
by Ol Lady   hen
-peckin my tail
feathers till i can't

~

the sun casts
long shadows
—a pair of rain
-bows so bright
    should steal em

            all night drags
the dark   thick
stars like lice

crow i god
    -da fly up
end the shadow

        moon's a wolf
eye starin me down

love season

If Gim*p* the Cr°w
True-loved Ol Lady
He no leave now
Stay long time   *maybe*

Loves seasons all
Leaves come then go
Gim*p* ain't only human
Just your base-sick crow

crow-made wine

find a bucket, pail, or barrel
        if you can't find one
        a wide puddle or deep ditch will do

fill your container half up with rain
        drop crab-apples in
aplipple plopple plup
bruised and rotting wind
fall work best   yank out enough
rhubarb stocks
        careful to discard the leaves
toss stocks into the mix
        don't mind no dirt
slup slopple aslipple

this is the basic recipe
        you may wish to experiment
after a few batches   add in
orange peels or yellow dandelions
remember   always keep one eye
out for loose compost lids

here's the hard part
        you will have to wait
                in a few short days
things should start to bubble
        means your work is
nearin fruition after

three or four weeks
your crow-made should
be ready to be
        enjoyed responsibly

don't drink and fly
        and be careful you don't face-
plant the bottom of your bucket
        lost a friend that way

Gim*p*'s Dream

In sleep Gim*p* dreams   black crow dream   two birds
sky horizon   blue deep ending   One bird's all black
the other's pure white   They fly   two trains same track

As they grow close the pair rise slow as summer
clouds brewing up storm   One bird could be dove
the other's crow   They fly theory   the apex of triangle

It's obvious they'll meet   the way some trains do

Afterwards
                    white and black feathers twist/twirl down
A magpie emerges from their convergence of tidings
glides solid wings down   lands with a flutter-skip
over snow   hops a bit   closer   blue tracks   A
beaked twig   small still green leaves   dropped
   lands plumb   snow   wiggles as if shaken
by breath   Roots worm their way through snow
      down earth
                              The moon   a skull sky holds

parting shot

Bad bye Gim*p* Cr^{o}w
Un great full duck
Go wander coop   Blow
Get lightning struck

Gim*p* means business

Gim*p* Cr^o^w
Scrap Flesh Dealer
Our spirit is willing when your flesh is weak
No corpse too small!

Gim*p* as hobo

Hey hang tight Gim*p*
See end caboose
Fold wings don't skimp
Leg might fly loose

Urge comes must eat
Crack open beak
Die eats complete
Fat bugs foul meat

Down wind aim high
When Nature speaks
Wise-guy advice
Re: takin leaks

postcard

caught Winnipeg fr-
eight car headin
out fast vast West

good-byer's remorse

Any crow'll grow lonely
Down dust sky roads
Feelin very only
Sun-dried toad

Need a little friend-
Ship'll pass age day
Before light ends
Life slips   *okay?*

postcard

crossed Port-
age la Prairie creak
in steel wheelin wheels

near the foothills

O trip be travel
Raw ride lure joy
Up wake gravel
Chunks slip ahoy

See saw galore
Eye ball what's down
Tilt wings dive soar
Caws echo sound

Heart's pure wing
All mind wild gyre
Love spins wind thin
Ends brittle desire

first sigh/t

1

        any magpie is
mighty pretty bird
        half white
half black
claw print word

2

it's as if
The Maker
        way back when
in the beginnin
hit some trouble
makin up
                mind—
doubts shimmer
by light
and by dark

as if
  unable
in the end
to decide

if de light was
any damn good

introductions

Crow known as Gimp
My name ain't bull

Shit leg lies limp
Awe   some trouble

Muddy Magpie
Pleased to meetcha

Good look on rye
Could eat, would beak ya

muddy's proposition

Let's rob some nest
Break fast eggs suck
Blue ones be best
Red sky swells luck

Bring down eagle
Feathers sky fly
Ain't quite legal
Giver best try

Cold cuts carcass
Cracks bones white clean
Red blood marks us
Delight full sheen

Dance beak two beak
Hip jazz hop fast
Lay muddy streak
Save love long last

Shakespeare's crow

Word bird world me
Sweet breath neath wing
Clear dark eyes see
Pair song two sing

Grant tree for nest
So crow-wed we'd be
Sun dapples breast
Lean on rook's key

Gim*p* writes a poem

Yeah down pluck stars
In squalls low light
Plug moon shine jar
Slick dark ken night

Wind straight feather
Past quiet nest
Stay up for never
No shut-eye rest

If she be my girl
Caws two pair sing
Kill whole damn world
Share all dead things

Ol Lady's lament

O love
's a broke wing a
well worn perch
an empty limb

un
echoed
my caws
among city trees

need two crow

craving always adventure
you windy weed
grow up
you're three
four winters old   time
you settle down
stop strutting

why cache the heart?
life means: we share

come play a part
one half of pair

the thirteenth hole

Caws Raven lives
Top lone tall pine
At thirteenth hole
So cozy, mine

Little mischief
Day in night out
Love lie loud lie
Two Feets do shout

No   can't complain
Guts daily bread
In land of plenty
Grows fat ass spread

Loan sum lone lie
Big sky old tree
Viewwingtastic
No one not see

When boredom rears
Big empty head
Rave seeks out fear
Miss chance plays dead

half-time show (Canad Inns Stadium)

Ladies and gentlemen, could you put hands together for
Little Ken and the Late Night Embers here tonight to play:
Drunk on Thee.

the guys at the bar don't understand
when your heart's this full you become the man
you're meant to be my missing piece
so puzzling how you complete me

chorus

sometimes it feels alright to know
i can hold you tight i could let you go
and if my heart should break in two
i'd keep the small, send the big one to you

chorus bridge

we'll find a way to make things work
some days i'll be a saint on others a jerk
and there'll be times we've had a few
how can i settle with you?

chorus

....

chorus:

don't stop serving me
never get   my fill   of you
so undeserving of love
what's a guy (like me) supposed to do?

bridge:

don't cut me off
can't you see?
it ain't the booze talking
i'm drunk on thee

the meeting

Hell! O! Gim*p*! Cr^{o}w!
What news my boy?
Your trip was how?
Discovered joy?

Late bum-leg lie?
Stay wise of trouble?
How fares Ol Lady?
Still burst your bubbles?

Last day's arrived
O knew you'd come
Hard year survived
A not-her one

I've asked Stuff news!
Beak no more words
So tell me who's
Your black/white bird

and where are ya now Gim*p* Cr^o^w?

ya flew off wide
to ward de sun
wingin out
for de sea

ya always get dis
tense round a b
out dis time—
unreasoned bull

maybe dis sea
son jump-starts he
art's itch for de light

could be why ya come
plain ya think ya need
a little far place   a ho
me to run from

but i know
how bad your
leg makes ya fly
makin no sense
of direction ya
goofy big arcs

so sure i'll be
waitin my love
    burnin
slow string

gonna smack thee de
ad   damn right
cross de he
                    ad

true as this crow flies

egg/balls

Now Caws Raven's
Far biggest three
Won't take no guff
Caws knows no need be

Takes what he wants
Fair reason's gain
Knows death ain't easy
Bottom food chain

Roosts on golf course
Sees egg/balls fly
Thinks: *Scramble! Eggs!*
When hit they die!

Eye awake kens
Swoop-scoop beaked-ball
Fuckin ravens!
Curse one curse all

three's a crow/d

well ain't you two
a pair   now us
be three   of
            a kin/d

one raven
                a crow
now this magpie eye
spy with my little i

what share we air

                all stand
at the edge of land
            where water
                begins
            not to end

where sun
            hungers
                far
                dark

Muddy's daydream

let's be sky
fly rain
    fly dream
dance empty mind

                let's find a tree
    one good strong branch
    crow-barred we'd see
in night's entrance

            come end of rain
  drop   flutter-shake-
off light
air shall arc
rain beau web-cawt

Cawsin Raven daydreams

Cr^{o}w blood die bird
Of much less soul
So caw shun words
Stay good side sold

Eye for one   know
No thing Gim*p* thinks
Rave ends parley show
Him belly of lynx

Vagabond heart
Each one for own
Nip bud die smart
Strong crack head stone

Ol Lady daydreams

O ebb bony
Lazy ass crow

Last time my love
Atones for our world
(Don't *please*, think of
Your self once girl)

Can't Gim*p* be true
Right one I plead
Of mine what's due
Why two not treed?

friend lie advice

You see Gim*p* Cr^o^w
The Two Feets rule
If don't know this
Wind up toy fool

Us birds not much
Play small small part
Serve us up dead
Fly quick if so smart

Dig deep our role
Under take task
It's why we are
In eating fast

To take not give
Here meaning lies
Our way is to live
Let others die

the story of Gim*p*'s mishap

you never told me
what happened   your leg
a dried up creek bed flowing nowhere
hanging loose as an apple ready for fall

it's a long story   once i tell ya ya can't ask me to tell it again
round time i met Ol Lady   painful to recall that day so full
as spring   ya know there was a time i didn't know her

one day i felt a kind of warmth or smelly wind   but that ain't it
next thing i know i have to follow her   be in the same tree
on the same branch   in sight   so i'll hear her call

were these two Two Feets   once a week they packed their car
full of food   took off   this food drove us off our nut   worse
when they came back   hoped for fresh garbage   not a bag

one day we're watchin the Two Feets from our elm and she beaks
i'm going for it   i beak *goin for what?*   she beaks *food* as down
she swoops   the trunk   time i get there she's got a beak full of
cherries   ever had cherries?   and flies back our elm

i stare at all the food   bags and bags of it ya understand
apples oranges pears cherries even a melon   can only take one
can't decide   she calls *CROW*   a sharp noise/pain
down on/through my leg   caw *bloody murder*   jaw-trapped
by the trunk slam   flap darkness   caged   pull   no way

light bright   can't see   outline of Two Feets holdin club
CROW she warns   i jump   pain so bad i   flip over mid air
land at the Two Feets' feet   she said the club hit me so hard
i flew twenty feet before i started to fly on my own
back up our elm   Two Feets laughin the way they do

she looks at what's left of my leg   beaks *O Gimp Crow*
your leg it's   looks in my eye   caws so hard i think she's
off her nut   you see   i had an orange stuck on my beak
    later she said   it was the orange
made her fall for me   really sealed the deal

Cawsin Raven takes Gim*p* to the Olympics

    see Two Feets go
chase round big Os

wolf on his own trail
snaps at his own tail

fox-quick they go on snow
sticks stuck to Two Feets,
two more at other ends

see them slide down hills

bump   bumps   flip flips

how they try to win
g air   be bird

reason we look down
on their envy of us

soliloquy

Speak well off wing
Hope none will hear
Ill words I spring
Close no one's ear

Snow job Gim*p* Cr^{o}w
Truck awestruck luck
Golf players plow
Dead sit tin duck

Head up frees way
Crave Mud my own
Chips fall where may
Two birds one stone

relation slips

Muddy Magpie's
One with-it bird
Beak quick red eye
Caws sharp as sword

Blue sky her home
Wind spreads wing tips
Horizon slides
Yet never up slips

Flies straight narrow
Point A point B
Prey wide open
Kills all she see

Alert she scrounge
Bone-cracker beak
When Mud no eat
Mud nasty speak

Now Gim*p* ain't used
To dark all night fun
Likes his still roost
Alone no One

Cawsin Raven shows Gim*p* his perch

here Gim*p*   perch on this metal fence   no
beak the other way   won't see nothing   yes
    better   see how Two Feets slide   sticks
under feet   ends of their wings
    what?   yes   another is strapped to their back
    i think a thunder stick   why?   Gim*p*
my dear   Two Feets are afraid of us

must go   now   for a time   small
thing Muddy needs done   no you
stay   watch Two Feets play

~

well ain't this one for the books
a crow and a raven
perched on the targets
at least no biathlete is ready to shoot
but here comes Megan Imrie
of Falcon Lake, Manitoba
        and good   there goes the raven
shoo crow shoo
    have we found the rule book?
nothing eh?   Megan's setting up for
her first shot   yes she sees the crow
precious seconds being wasted here
how stupid can this bird be?
finger squeezes trigger
BLAM
she's got her first target

and there goes Gim*p*
lightning flying
out his ass

what the crow said

Who think thou art?
Dry twig dull peck
Black boggy fart
Pluck eye fly speck

O limp prick wag
Dead wind blind stench
Know wing proud brag
Lay off this wench

Don't steal life's light
Sweep Mud off feet
Eyes soar for sight
Tale up dead meat

Muddy daydreams

Babble wee rant
Dry up cloud sky
Oblige my want
Each day good die

You thick slur love
Eddy cross wind
Bright sun above
Arcs blind-dumb din

Gim*p* Crow's got stuff
Plumps red full blood
I sky swell luff
Cold feet sink mud

break up

Caws Rave's Old Boy
Faves good bad stuff
Games play-birds toy
Fine things turn rough

Strong beak shellac
Bone marrow nice
Snake sharp attack
Spring river's ice

Muddy Magpie's dream

Muddy Magpie sees
wet forest dreams
rain heat

a tree ever
green in a desert

she dreams white
clouds black sky white
sun black moon white snow
black ice white desert
black swamp white yin
black yang
t
his
ever
green
tr
ee

she dreams she flies
the empty zone
between the 10,
000 oppo-
sites of this world

mirrored along a thin
spine of wings p-
aired like lifelong mates

she dreams snow
clumps an evergreen

dreams the sky rains
pine cones   the tiny see-
ds within   fall   without a
sound   like hail on grass   or w-
heat in a grain elevator raising s-
low as bread   or water near
the end of the world

Muddy dreams she is horizon

Cawsin Raven's dream

Caws Rave dreams The Flood   great blue water
slowly rising   tree trunks/limbs/tops   till
water covers the whole whole earth and waves touch
sky   He dreams of a perch   any sign of land

This is his Flying Dream   the one he dreams
each sleep   In it he high-skies above water
stretching all distance   seeing no tree he knows
Only the lip of horizon   where light/dark begins/ends
And   he must keep flying   if he falls he'll be
swallowed   Alone   he   sees   no other

A whiteness drifts the sky like cloud   She beaks
a twig of small green leaves   Here is where
again he must decide: Shall he follow to where
she totes the twig?   or trace her path back to land?

Once more he feels it start   two pairs of wings
near his heart   At first the tear seems
painless as an old memory of death   soon
the cleft widens along his spine   Four wings
flap against each other   the double-yolked
of one shell   And Raven is no longer
a raven but two crows   One flies
for the white bird   the other
    for what may be land

❍l Lady's dream

inside her head ❍l Lady sees elm-arched streets
barrel-round trunks   branches fork   a high nest
made of sticks and mud and thorn   She dreams eggs
a small heart-clutch   She dreams the other face
of the shy moon   She dreams water

f   g
a   n
l i
l s
l a p p i n g
r   n
g

on/off thick limbs   against burled trunks   over bare
roots   She dreams water seeps in through the sticks
and mud and thorn   flows up around and over her
eggs rise the nest to float on the birdless surface

Heart-torn
she dreams one ocean   far as eye can see
last crow on an ark of thin stick, wet mud,
sharp thorn

death of Muddy Magpie

Teed up egg/ball
Golf club's black swing
Gim*p* seize not 't all
Dumb ding-a-ling

Mud's derring-do
Mite chance live it
Slow Mud falls to
Death neath divot

Caws Raven laments Muddy

No return caws
Breath broke out head
Club gave her pause
Cracked Mud lies dead

It should be Gim*p*
Down still groan cool
Got no symp-
Athy for fool

Best laid plans of
Mice or and duck
Is true with love
We all up fuck

retreat

Gim*p* Cr^{o}w   no know
Ol Lady's   faith
Why true   love glows
For him not   sayth

Gim*p* Cr^{o}w knows   no
Reason be dis   grace
Bets wind   place show
Saves ass   about-face

postcards

rest Crows
nest Pass, next loop de
loop O Kam
l
oops

took Medicine
Hat, off stamped-
ed Calgary

flew on dry air
smoked past
Brand-
on

the return of Gim*p* Cr^{o}w

Crow?   dat you Gim*p*?
Blew back dis tense
Thought One too simple
Threw off pretense

What's dat ya beak?
Green twig be carried?
Love's nest ya seek?
Crow-wed married?

countin crows

(few years have gone by)

1

  one egg
  two egg
three egg
                four

touch down talon
don't right lie know
this dumb crow
don't count
no more

2

ya know father
-hood's a hard
shell to crack

once eggs
pop o
          pen can't
lay 'em back

little gimp goes on and on on how Gim*p* Cr^{o}w goes on and on

my Old Crow always on and on about the good old days
    how lanes used to pile up with garbage
high as the eye could eye
back before recyclin   when
all ya had to do was tip a lid
and bingo   there's supper

on and on   how in late summer
smell was to die for   so i ask him
why would you die for a smell?
no smell i know will fill your belly

he doesn't hear me or isn't saying
beaks instead of Garbage Hill

there's this hill of garbage high as the sky
sometimes you'd find so many maggots
ya couldn't eat 'em all

i tell you he's losing it   big time   gob
drooling off his beak with the mere memory
of maggots   The Myth of Garbage Hill

says *i'll take you there you'll see yourself*

so we fly over   and top of this fat hill
there's a fence to keep the road and cars in
green grass and trees   picnic tables and fire pits
dogs and their Two Feets doing what they always do
garbage bins   don't see or smell much

so where's all this garbage?
lead me to your maggots and Old Crow
looks about him *it was here right here* he
beaks *losing it* i mind and home fly

little gimp muses on names

why do we have names?

a crow is a crow is a crow is a crow
isn't this true?   aren't we all
        all the same crow? One
in terms of crow consciousness

a crow can never be raven
a raven will never be crow
we see the difference
know our flock

same thing for ducks since
a duck is a duck is a duck is a duck
ducks don't get mixed up   ducks know
the heart of their duckness
        don't argue about how much
they fail to measure up to some i
deal duck   for them everything's ducky

when we start to give each other
names   things change

take my Old Crow
called Gim*p* Crow be caws of his leg
our Ol Lady named him
and the naming changed him

and i   i am Young Crow
named little gimp by my Old Crow
called Snowball by my Old Lady Crow

name me change me re
arrange me   strange me

little gimp on his name

i ask you who wants to be a chip off the Old Crow?
what kind of crow gives their son his own name
ego?   you betcha   vanity too
Old Crow's the one with the bum-leg
so calling me little gimp makes no sense
a curse is what it is this name   a blue
pain in the ass is what being number two is
Old Crow yaks *you're the beginnin of my line*
well *hello?* i want to get off his line
it's his hang up not mine

thing too is Old Lady
Crow calls me Snowball

out of the blue Old Crow beaks
let's go out and win one for the Gimper
or he'll crow something sounds like Two Feets
I went down to St. James Infirmary
I saw my Sweetheart there.
i haven't a clue what he's on about
my little whimper he calls me
my little juicy pimple
my little smiling dimpler
my simple little gimper
my sunny summer little jumping imper
so on and on he goes
        losing it is what i call it

and all his feathers turning
grey in a slow grey wind

Ol Lady is worried

come here Snowball i'm worried about our Gimp
of late he acts strange   can't say it's too much
crow-made   though he does go at it head
-first from time to time

you mean him beakin Two Feets?

so you've heard him too
oh yeah: *Get six gamblers to carry my coffin.*
Six chorus girls to sing my song.
he's not cawing   tweets sweet as a robin

right out of the blue   no reason
maybe he's unaware he does it

where does your Old Crow go
each Flyday night?   pretends to be
asleep   dreaming his nightmare

he told me how his leg

got trapped

yes

used to give him bad dreams
now i think he fakes 'em

why?

i think your Old Crow's
being tamed by a Two Feets
    Snowball   follow him to
-night   see where he goes

little gimp asks his Old Crow

what's the difference between a cage and a trap?

with one you know you're dead
with the other you'll wish you were

but aren't we all caged
in our body the bones
our flesh and blood
don't you have a sense
of being trapped within so
me thing we're unable to leave
no matter how hard we flap
our wings or tongues
       be
        hind

ya mean my leg?

no not exactly there's
the question of hatching

caws some say being egged
is one stage hatching out
  the next after we die we be
come egg again or will join sky

hard to say eh
since i'm not
dead yet

At the Viscount Gort Hotel

On the smokers' patio, a little after midnight. Gimp perches the back of an empty chair. Enter little gimp, stage Up.

and what are *you* doin here?

❍l Lady sent me to keep an eye on you
thinks you fake your asleep-flying
wants to know where you go
what you do   is worried

can take care of myself

what about your Two Feets beak?

that's my singin   have to practise
don't i?   can't ya hear their music?

typical Two Feets no sense

I went back to see my baby
And great God she was lying there dead.

and what does *that* mean?

it's beyond meanin   a Two Feets song is like
a bright red robin in spring   so sad
beakin for a mate   and so full of hope
once you've heard it   enough
times   she'll just fly out

❍l Lady thinks
a Two Feets is taming you

it's more the other
way round   watch

Gim*p* jumps up and is off
begins a low slow circling of the patio
caw *caw* *caw* *caw*
a Two Feets in a Goldeyes baseball cap
spots Gim*p* leaves his near empty
beer bottle on a nearby table steps
back Gim*p* lands on the table
flutter-skips stops at the bottle
beaks its lip and tilts
back the beer
dry Two Feets laugh
Gim*p* shakes off the bottle
hops back up in air
lands back on the back of his chair

okay i ask you
who's tamin who?

what's in those bottles?

it's crow-made but clouds higher

i've never tried crow-made

really? okay i'm your father so here's the deal
but maybe yes it'll be easier if i show ya
see de juicy lime bottom of that bottle?
get it for ya so ya can have a snort

Gim*p* sw
oops down   beak-lips the clear
bottle   tilts it back   and oh
look   something
ain't right here

Gim*p* slumps   over   the edge of the table
down to the patio floor   wings all a twitching
breast pumping air   eyes turning blue
bum-leg still as river ice

little gimp lands by his side
tries to beak-break the bottle   no go
pulls Gim*p* hard by his feathers
get his neck the heck out of the neck
again no go   nothing but feathers

meanwhile the Two Feets
gather round   point and laugh

little gimp turns to them
wings spread out and turned up
asks: *great God?*

the Two Feets in the Goldeyes cap
grabs Gim*p*   pulls the beer
bottle off his beak
lays Gim*p* gently back
down on the patio floor   steps back

little gimp returns to his father
sees the blackness return to Gim*p*'s eyes
the lime wedged on the tip of his beak

too many crows

in each vacant lot i look
  crows peck to pick
    up dry scrub
      grubs

  near a dusty corner at the lake
 crows gather to block the way
point thin beaks like fingers

daily on the local news
a row of dead crows
laid out on a stain
-less steel table—
ungraceful after
-math of autopsy

  lazy slice of over
-head wings heard
passing a grave

once again
CBC Late Night
shows Hitchcock's *The Birds*

and it's easy to get spooked
thinking they might know
something's going on
on to the no good i'm up to
me dipping my pen
using their ink-
black feathers

crow as image
in want of an author

    rules of a game
i've stumbled up
on   how i
try to be
            content
with the ink i spread

epitaph

True Gim*p* loved her
Good-natured caws
Book time be over
Now your applause

Acknowledgments and Thanks

I started writing *Gimp Crow* after noticing a crow with a twisted leg hanging around my neighbourhood. The leg seemed to give the crow a personality. The first one was: "daybreaks." I wrote it the night before the 9/11 acts.

There are always many people to thank. Here they are:

Heather Boyd – for listening and sharing
phyllis cherrett – for your critical eye
Dennis Cooley – for being my editor
Gloe Cormie – for your friendship
Catherine Hunter – for helping me get out of my basement
Olya Marko – for speaking our blood
Ben McArthur – for Salisbury House on Sundays
Leslie Mundwiler – for the books: mine, yours and others
Brian J. Pannell – for starting the group
Leon Rooke – for the grant
Halia Stolar – for your rhymes
St. Peter's Abbey – for time, silence and food
Bernadette Wagner – for asking: what are you writing?

The staff and regulars at Playmaker's Polo Park
The staff and regulars at the Viscount Gort
The staff and owners of Turnstone Press

Many of the poems were written while under a Writers B grant awarded to the author by the Manitoba Arts Council. Thanks.

An extra special thank you goes out to Olya Marko. Her beautiful painting *Beaconia by Daylight* (acrylic, mixed media, 2010) is the image used for the cover.